A Bat Ca...

By Liza Charlesworth

ISBN: 978-1-339-02683-1

Art Director: Tannaz Fassihi; Designer: Tanya Chernyak
Photos © Getty Images.
Copyright © Liza Charlesworth. All rights reserved. Published by Scholastic Inc.

3 4 5 6 7 8 9 10   68   32 31 30 29 28 27 26 25 24

Printed in Jiaxing, China. First printing, August 2023.

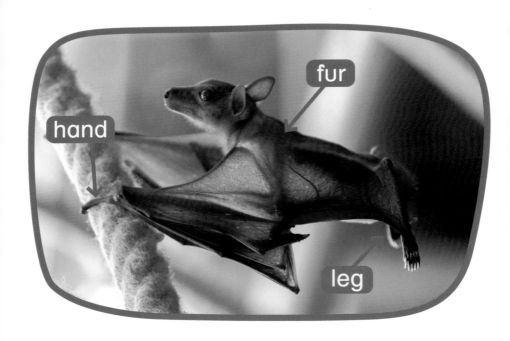

It is a bat!
A bat has hands and legs.
A bat has fur.

Flap, flap, flap!
A bat can be black.
It can be red or tan.

Bats can flap so fast.
See it go. Zip, zap!

Bats snack on plants.

Bats snack on bugs.

Can bats get wet? Yes!
A bat can swim a bit.

Bats say, "Click, click!"
They can grip sticks.
In the day, they get rest.

A bat is not a pest.
A bat is the best!